Copyright © 2020 by M.S. Wordsmith

All rights reserved.

No part of this book may be reproduced in any form or by any electronic or mechanical means, including information storage and retrieval systems, without written consent of the copyright holder, except for the use of brief quotations in a book review.

Set Yourself Up for Success

ABOUT ME

I'm a coach for writers and other creatives, an editor, a writer, an intuitive healer, and a custom retreat organiser. Born in the Netherlands and raised by my Dutch mother and Scottish expat father, I moved to the island of Cyprus in February 2019.

The thing about being somewhere new is that it sheds a different light on your life. Your mind opens up to other perspectives, and you find yourself brimming with new ideas. Or old ideas you never wanted to take seriously suddenly demand your attention.

Bringing the spiritual into my work was a scary step for me, because I've always tried to keep the two separate. I say 'tried' because quite a few of my clients, and the work they brought with them, have forced me to merge my professional background with my spiritual interests. Some hired me to edit or translate their holistic books, others came to me for coaching and were struggling in a way that needed a broader approach. And then there are the many writers and other creatives who are openly incorporating spirituality into their practice as we speak.

Over the past year, I've switched gears and gradually allowed the spiritual to enter my workspace. This book is one of its many manifestations. It goes without saying that I hope you'll enjoy it, and get from it everything you need.

Mariëlle S. Smith

INTRODUCTION

Welcome to *Set Yourself Up for Success*, a 31-day tarot challenge for writers and other creatives ready to have their best year yet.

Initially designed as a tarot challenge for Instagram, the thirty-one daily prompts in this book will help you get a firm grasp on the year ahead, whenever that new year starts for you. Perhaps it's on the first of January or your birthday, or on that random day in the middle of September you decide it's time to get your act together and become serious about where you're going.

During this challenge, you will set your goals and intentions for the next year as you reflect on:

- the year that has come and gone, including the lessons and victories,
- where you are now creatively, and
- the challenges and opportunities for growth you will face in the twelve months ahead.

No good ride will ever be a smooth one, but if we know where we're headed and how to best deal with the obstacles to come, the ride can't be but a success. Just buckle up, hit that accelerator, and enjoy ;)

Doing a tarot challenge*

So, how does a tarot challenge work? Quite simply, actually. Each day, you pick up your deck of choice, shuffle to your heart's content, and pick a card or more, depending on the question and what your gut tells you. The next day, you put the card(s) back into your deck, shuffle like you mean it, and pull out your next draw.

Even though each day in this book implies the amount of cards you could be drawing, there's no reason you should follow that advice. Your gut always knows best. Likewise, it doesn't matter to me how you shuffle your cards or decide which card is the one that needs picking. Just go with what you've been taught or feels right for you in this moment. There's really no doing this wrong.

The same goes with how you interpret the cards' messages. Some feel utterly comfortable using the guidebook that came with their deck, while others rely solely on their intuition. You can do either or a bit of both: when doing a reading, I don't mind glancing at the description offered by the creator of the cards, especially when I feel there is more to a card but I just can't seem to grasp the full meaning of it at the time. The guidebook won't always bridge that gap, but it might just give you another perspective, that 'Aha, of course!' moment that will kickstart your intuition. Whatever you do, don't let others tell you what is right and wrong: there's only a right and wrong for you, and you will know what is what in the moment.

I highly suggest that you write down your findings and reflect on them as you go. The same card might show up again and again: what could that mean? Some cards will only make sense later, after you answer a few more questions. Reflecting on previous draws will be especially relevant in those cases. And, even if all the cards make perfect sense the moment you draw them, looking at the bigger picture might still reveal something you had not considered before. It's in the reflecting that the wisdom lies.

Use whatever works for you

Those familiar with my work know that I don't differentiate between means of divination. I might use the word tarot, but you can use any deck of cards, whether that be tarot, oracle, or angel. If you'd rather use your crystals or your runes, feel free to go with that.

For those who want to do the challenge but aren't comfortable using either of those divinitory tools, or simply don't own any, use each question as a journal prompt. Sit down in a quiet space, take a few deep breaths, and let whatever answers need to bubble to the surface come.

Likewise, if you would like to mix things up—perhaps the one question makes you want to grab your favourite oracle deck, while another makes you pick up a notebook—please do. Your challenge, your rules. As long as you follow that gut of yours.

DAY 1

How can I best sum up my creative self over the past twelve months?

DAY 2

In what areas did I grow most as a creative over the past year?

DAY 3

What is the main lesson my creative self has been learning over the past twelve months?

DAY 4

How has this lesson changed me as a creative already?

DAY 5

How will this lesson change me even further in the year to come?

DAY 6

What has held me back the most creatively over the past twelve months?

DAY 7

What have I been ignoring about my creative self over the past year?

DAY 8

What has been my biggest creative milestone or victory of these past twelve months?

DAY 9

What milestones and victories will carry me into the next twelve months of my creative life?

DAY 10

How will these milestones and victories carry me into the next year?

DAY 11

Where am I now creatively?

DAY 12

How can I remain centred and in touch with my inner muse as the past twelve months make way for a new year?

DAY 13

What are my creative goals and intentions for the next three months?

DAY 14

What is the main challenge I will face as a creative during this period (1) and how can I best go about it (2)?

DAY 15

What lesson(s) must I learn during this period to ensure growth?

DAY 16

What mindset will help me turn the next quarter into a success?

DAY 17

What are my creative goals and intentions for the next four to six months?

DAY 18

What is the main challenge I will face as a creative during this period (1) and how can I best go about it (2)?

DAY 19

What lesson(s) must I learn during this period to ensure growth?

DAY 20

What mindset will help me turn the next four to six months into a success?

Day 21

What are my creative goals and intentions for the next seven to nine months?

DAY 22

What is the main challenge I will face as a creative during this period (1) and how can I best go about it (2)?

DAY 23

What lesson(s) must I learn during this period to ensure growth?

DAY 24

What mindset will help me turn the next seven to nine months into a success?

DAY 25

What are my creative goals and intentions for the next ten to twelve months?

DAY 26

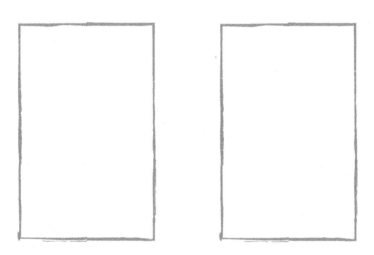

What is the main challenge I will face as a creative during this period (1) and how can I best go about it (2)?

DAY 27

What lesson(s) must I learn during this period to ensure growth?

Day 28

What mindset will help me turn the next ten to twelve months into a success?

DAY 29

What is the overall theme for the year to come?

DAY 30

What do I need to keep reminding myself of as the next twelve months of my creative life unfold?

DAY 31

What other advice must I take to heart to turn the year ahead into my most successful creative year yet?

A QUICK FAVOUR

I hope this book brought you everything you needed.

If you liked it and it was in any way helpful, can I ask you for a quick favour?

Authors are nowhere without honest reviews, and I'd truly appreciate it if you left one on Amazon, Goodreads, or my Facebook page facebook.com/mswordsmith.

OTHER BOOKS BY ME

Available on Amazon and Kindle Unlimited

https://www.amazon.com/dp/B07W7D8S53

If you enjoy tarot, self-work, and are a creative, then this book is for you. I was part of the test group during its writing, and when I heard that the project had been published, just had to pick up a copy, so I could do the entire 31 days all over again later. The questions, day to day, follow intuitively, and the insights stack, day to day, following a logical progression of examination. Whether you read the cards spiritually, or as a way of helping yourself think through life questions, this book is still for you. No dogma, no airy-fairy here, just straight up questions that evoke honest answers, all leading towards a creative, productive life of deeper satisfaction and purpose. A couple of suggestions: do the questions as written and journal each day's answer! That way you get the most out of the exercises.

Beth Annette on Amazon

OTHER BOOKS BY ME

Available on Amazon and Kindle Unlimited

https://www.amazon.com/dp/B07WSGQRPS/

I didn't have a specific project in mind when I picked up this book, but there are plenty of spreads that give practical advice for current works. What I did use are the spreads for getting in touch with what you are called to create, getting in touch with the Muse, creative blocks—the big Artist's Spread at the end of the book really gave me a new perspective. Even though you can dip in and out with each numbered spread, this book really guides you on a journey from discovering what you want to create, what might stand in your way, troubleshooting the project, and moving on to your next work. I used both tarot and oracle cards, and got great readings with both. I'm a writer, but this book would be great for all types of creatives; it's about connecting with your intuition.

Michelle M on Amazon

OTHER BOOKS BY ME

Available on Amazon and Kindle Unlimited

https://www.amazon.com/dp/B07ZDKR8MY

Fleshing Out the Narrative: A 31-Day Tarot and Journal Challenge for Writers is designed to help you more fully understand: your story and characters; the most important story elements at play in your work; how these elements interact; and how they can best move the story forward.

Fleshing Out the Narrative walks you through thirty-one days of questions that will help you investigate: the premise, the theme, the hook, the setting, the main character, the antagonist, the confidant(e), the foil, and the mentor.

If you could use some divinatory help developing and expanding on your outline and story ideas, this is the book for you, whether you're into tarot, oracle, or angel cards, crystals, runes, or prefer to journal.

OTHER BOOKS BY ME

Available on Amazon and Kindle Unlimited

https://www.amazon.com/dp/B081Y6ZMPY

- Do you struggle with setting goals that reflect your daily reality?
- Do you want to practise breaking goals down into manageable chunks?
- Would you like more insight into your writing habit(s) and figure out why you keep getting in your own way?
- And do you want to create a sustainable writing practice that honours your needs and desires as a writer?

Then the *52 Weeks of Writing Author Journal and Planner* is for you.

52 Weeks of Writing brings together every lesson I have learned as a writing coach, editor, and writer. Wary as I am of comparisonitis and unhealthy competition, this author journal and planner was designed to help you develop and fine-tune a practice that works for you.

If you're ready to get out of your own way and become the writer you're meant to be, pick up your copy of the *52 Weeks of Writing Author Journal and Planner* today.

OTHER BOOKS BY ME

Available on Amazon and Kindle Unlimited

https://www.amazon.com/dp/B07ZDKR8MY

Fleshing Out the Narrative: A 31-Day Tarot and Journal Challenge for Writers is designed to help you more fully understand: your story and characters; the most important story elements at play in your work; how these elements interact; and how they can best move the story forward.

Fleshing Out the Narrative walks you through thirty-one days of questions that will help you investigate: the premise, the theme, the hook, the setting, the main character, the antagonist, the confidant(e), the foil, and the mentor.

If you could use some divinatory help developing and expanding on your outline and story ideas, this is the book for you, whether you're into tarot, oracle, or angel cards, crystals, runes, or prefer to journal.

OTHER BOOKS BY ME

Available on Amazon and Kindle Unlimited

https://www.amazon.com/dp/B081Y6ZMPY

- Do you struggle with setting goals that reflect your daily reality?
- Do you want to practise breaking goals down into manageable chunks?
- Would you like more insight into your writing habit(s) and figure out why you keep getting in your own way?
- And do you want to create a sustainable writing practice that honours your needs and desires as a writer?

Then the *52 Weeks of Writing Author Journal and Planner* is for you.

52 Weeks of Writing brings together every lesson I have learned as a writing coach, editor, and writer. Wary as I am of comparisonitis and unhealthy competition, this author journal and planner was designed to help you develop and fine-tune a practice that works for you.

If you're ready to get out of your own way and become the writer you're meant to be, pick up your copy of the *52 Weeks of Writing Author Journal and Planner* today.

Contact

There are different ways and places to contact me:

Website: mswordsmith.nl
E-mail: marielle@mswordsmith.nl
Instagram: instagram.com/mariellessmith
Facebook: facebook.com/mswordsmith

To receive updates and stay in the loop, sign up to my newsletter and get a free 3-day exercise to overcome limiting beliefs:

eepurl.com/dvCQkX

Made in the USA
Coppell, TX
27 January 2020